Following Rivers in Trees

Also by Adèle Ogiér Jones and published by Ginninderra Press

Poetry

Afghanistan – waiting for the bus
From the Edge of the Pacific
Beyond the Blackbird Field
Counting the Chiperoni
Sense of Place (Pocket Poets)
Blantyre Leaves (Pocket Poets)

Fiction

Desert Diya

Adèle Ogiér Jones

Following Rivers in Trees

Acknowledgements

'Travellers' first presented as 'The Bus' in *Sense of Place*,
Ginninderra Press Pocket Poets, 2014
'Jet Stream', 'To Seamus Heaney', 'Declan's well', 'Friends',
'Music at the corner pub' and 'Betty's apple' in *Sense of Place*,
Ginninderra Press Pocket Poets, 2014
'Standing stones' and 'Solstice foraging'
in *Lothlorien Poetry Journal*, 2021
'From Eavan Boland's "Anna Liffey"' in *Eavan Boland, New Collected Poems*, W.W. Norton, 2008

Following Rivers in Trees
ISBN 978 1 76109 367 8
Copyright © text Adèle Ogiér Jones 2022
Cover image: Oliver Nares

First published 2022 by
GINNINDERRA PRESS
PO Box 3461 Port Adelaide 5015
www.ginninderrapress.com.au

Contents

An Laoi – River Lee

Listening to the river	11
Along the quays	12
St Francis in Cork	13
Travellers	14
Women's tales	15
Jet stream	16
Quaker lane teahouse	17
Spring	19
Body Corporate	20
Sandbags at the gallery	22
Crawford lace makers	23
Cork arts foyer	24
To Seamus Heaney	25
Blackberry summer chutney	26
Bank holiday in Ireland	28
Dublin bus strike	29
Grand silence	31
Searching trees	33
Endangered species	35
The 237	36
Rendezvous	37
Poster at the station	38
Food for the dreamer	39
Labyrinth	40

An Bhrid – River Bride

The Bride from the Lee	45
Brigid's track	46
Lost story	47

Otter on the Bride	49
By rivers	51
Snowdrops	52
Sonnet for a storm	53
New dreaming	54
Light through the window	55
Searching for Bride	56
Sign to Kildare	57
Question	59
Near Bride's abbey	60
Bulldozed convent	61

An Abhainn Mhór – River Blackwater

Where the Bride meets the Blackwater	65
The Blackwater	67
Thistledown	68
Pilgrimage	69
Midleton	70
That faerie queen	71
In Tara's halls	72
Where rushes grow	74
Declan's well	75
Ardmore	76
Presence	77
Frigate	78
The Helen	79
At the clock tower	82
Youghal lighthouse	83
Old photos	84
Connectivity	87

Abhainn na Bandan – River Bandon

Climbing trees	91
The bride at Broken Creek	92
Finding Coill Mhura	94
At the end of a side road	99
Kilvurra stones	101
Bandon	102
Bus stop	103
Rock hard	104
Storytelling	105
In a field	106
Standing stones	107
Solstice foraging	108

An Aighlinn – River Ilen

Ilen	111
Sunday morning	112
Friends	114
Next door to Forge House	115
Dandelion down	116
Reflecting rain	117
Haiku on Skibbereen Bridge	118
Where otters greet the Ilen	119
Sonnet at Mizen	120
Woodland garden – Liss Ard	121
At the poetry marathon	122
After the hunger film	123
Music at the corner pub	124
At Forge House	125
Convent for sale	126
For rent	127
Festival windows	128

Autumn foraging	129
Gathering berries	130
Sentinel	131
Reen Peninsula	132
For Annie Sullivan	133
Betty's apple	134
Fire	135
Soup kitchen	136
Topaz	137
On the river	138
Rosscarbery memory	139
A voice	140
From Eavan Boland's 'Anna Liffey'	141

An Laoi – River Lee

– a river which rises in the Shehy Mountains on the western border of County Cork and flows eastwards through Cork, where it splits in two for a short distance, creating an island on which the city centre is built, then passing through Cork Harbour on the south coast, one of the largest natural harbours in the world, to empty into the Celtic Sea.

>listening to rivers
>flowing resigned through old trees
>escape predicted
>to ancient coastlines unchanged
>by seas of wild storms

Listening to the river

Can I entice you
    to where a winter embrace
awaits love's passion
        to that place in the reeds
        where waterbirds stand
outside the grey lounge room
into late season's soft sky
        out from the comfort of home
        to morning's newness
away from screens, to vistas
unfolding this dawn
        from predictability
        to crisp mysteries
from cosy comforts indoors
to where winter waits
        with promises to calm thoughts
        weighed down without sun
to where ravens drop stolen
nuts for cars crushing
        outside mind's confusion
        to see distant highlands
to the changing riverside
where herons wait still
        to the newly mown farm fields
        where cormorants stand proud
from yesterday's memories
to the noon's brief warmth
        to the beckoning mountain
        white standing silent
above the hushed fog
where the river warbles on.

Along the quays

An otter scampers
When all is quiet
        Down along the river
          Where the brown trout swim
And the kingfisher waits
Hidden low and bright
Watching from the reeds left from
Ages past, hiding stones
Hewn strong to hold the waters back.

She dashes to the boats
Moored firm
        Waiting the storm's return
          Searching for forgotten scraps
From fish the boys and men have cleaned
Before the market claims and pays
Or if she has no chance to claim this night
It's to another place, perhaps a frog
Who waits too long, observing.

A coat of grey in evening
Light soft
        Russet near to dawn, in boulders
          Near the footings of each bridge
Grass tussocks be her seat, a couch
Her denning site, hidden underground
Where she weaves her busy tales
With other life surviving city daily refuse
Debris of the life above oblivious to her ways.

St Francis in Cork

Did St Francis visit Cork?
though not sainted then,
would he have laughed out
loud and long to think of it,
a simple man perhaps
like the old man sitting
at the counter in the side lane bar
today,

chatting with whomsoever
sits beside him
to share his bottle of dark brew
bought to wash the three-course meal
with bread and wine and tea,
his bottle large to supplement
the cravings and a friendship
with any passing by,

some from town,
with others all alone, dejected
till they see his lonely smile
reflecting their secret need,
calling out
it beckons with a healing
and the comfort found in
sharing a glass or two,

just as Francis would have done
if he had visited another tapas bar
far down a hidden lane,
in those years so long ago
meeting people who dreamt a friend
with simple words and greeting.

Travellers

Dublin city centre
says the man who looks as if he'd fit as well into Mumbai's heart,
two smooth red-lipped girls who'd be at home in Melbourne
Guangzhou, or Hong Kong's ports,
a self-confessed antipodean claiming Cork's distant roots
looks right, accent not.
        Across an aisle
computer balanced on knees of a long-legged man
feet searching space round a suitcase crammed below,
book held in artist's hands a rare sight
where ipads and phones are tapped
in tense anticipation.
        Sedentary travellers
napping as day breaks slowly
while the world flies past,
nothing shared, no stories for still grey
clouds on a pale horizon, lonely
silent greeting for a pregnant shallow sun.

Women's tales

There is an old lady on the bus to Killarney
says the first line scrawled in a notebook,
no more sadly, too far back
too many stories to remember her words
though they would have been
remarkable.

Reminded again on yesterday's bus down from Dublin
a woman now sad that hospitality has gone,
those times have passed, she said
all different now
things changing so fast
too many gone to too many lands,
things once unheard of, now acceptable
talk shows on things churches once promulgated.

Her furious reliance on storm weather news
ipad messages predicting the future
hoping these make up for repeated
disappointments
unprecedented details exposed
in late remembering.

Jet stream

We can blame it on the jet stream
it could have blown us over if we'd let it
headlines in next day's paper
and business section announcing
at wild parties, even good girls get into trouble.

Indiscriminate, taking all in its path
rolling forty-five-ton trucks like matchbox toys
across the highway
blocking cars and trucks and buses on the Dublin route
wildest party heard of for many years.

There are old men though, talking confident that we'll listen,
those of nineteen eighty or forty-nine were fierce ones
I remember, one says, because that was the night
my wife became with child again
that night, the grandest of them all.

Quaker lane teahouse

Faces lining walls gaze down,
Look out vacantly
Postmodern loneliness speaks
From eyes unfocused.
Others concentrate on corner screens
Ochre, greens into grey
More suited to eucalypts
Emerald shades missing
From this old cinema now teahouse
Far before its namesake.

Fellini old Italian in the Quaker quarter
Where faces grey and pinched
In the cold long before
The focus of eyes looking out
At need and desperation
Small cemetery two buildings further down the lane
Ignored by warm pedestrians on the lookout
For coffee and teas of different kinds.

Sweets too numerous to name.
Titles from afar, Tunisian orange
In other places Moroccan,
Totally expected scones and jam for those
Fed on sugar, colonists growing
Rich on chocolate and cocoa
Replaced by cocaine in back streets
Stories too numerous most choose to forget.

Near the tea house in the side lane
Off Patrick's street
Sense of place evades the lounge
Like smoke from snuffed candles
Invisible, silent
Lingering for those aware.

Spring

A spring has escaped across the tiled floor
laid out so recent
dulled by fancy architraves above
spring here since Brigid's day,
old Imbolc disappearing
forgotten in storms thrashing inland.

Pen without spring a challenge for writing
a lone poem thrashing, lashing the soul to escape
to be written here in the lane of the Carey's
and the Quakers before them
now at Fellini's familiar wayside stop
where women quietly chat, free at this time of day.

Where a lone young man stands under eaves
dripping outside, sheltering from rain
pleading with those passing by
fresh days pass swamped by torrents
uncommon for this time of year
as buds showing fruitfulness sink

In drowning, crops due for sowing before her feast
six months hence when the virgin disappears
making ready for crops birthing
all must be prepared
but how can this happen without spring
like this moment's few verses with just a thimble of ink.

Body Corporate

Two Irish lads in number seven
then three, and four for a time
neighbours happy enough
though it was always *the Irish boys*
from those whose roots lay elsewhere
smug offspring from the other side.

    Then their parties, late night celebrations
    after midnight return from jobs committed
    labouring, service, cash and more later
    yet wine enough behind closed doors
    at quiet celebrations in neighbouring homes,
    UEFA soccer late here and with it drinks and cheering.

Then all seemed fine again
their mourning with the tens of thousands watching
Melbourne's farewell funeral prayer
emotion for the former Dublin lad
Aussie football with its players bonded tightly
one creed through single language united.

    Commiserations to occupants from number seven
    handshakes offered as if he'd been their man
    Ireland's proud son their own brother
    but as soon as this was over, forgotten
    complaints again, noise coming through a wall
    where plants and weeds reached over.

Nature's own threatening to cross
over the harsh concrete wall
dividing one patch of forgotten garden
unkempt, uncontrolled, ignored
by regularity adjacent, three feet by twelve
watered, trimmed, tidy, predictable.
>	Then four Irish lads pared down to three
>	in keeping with occupancy rate
>	quiet, unseen, only footsteps on the pavement
>	no cigarette butts
>	nothing to disturb
>	deathly quiet.

Sandbags at the gallery

Daffodils will not last beyond snow
in glass bottles for camphor
or syrup for winter,
blackberry juice and orange water
so sweet for summer
lie waiting for spring,
flasks washed away
in rain's flooding
sandbags saturated sink down
heavy against locked doors.

A gallery of faces viewing others
sip coffee,
reminiscing
collections growing older on each level,
token paintings, common themes
remembered on cold, damp winter nights
icy reminiscences
skate early on mornings
frozen till warmth thaws
a new era.

Crawford lace makers

Lace makers in photographs
rich hair piled high, bent over bobbins
and needlepoint, dressed warmly
unrelated to sisters of presentation
in temples for desolate girls
with dry fingers cracked in the cold
unwanted in houses where fires
boasted loud
wealthy and bold in grey stone
near hearths saved only for warmth
of the few
gathering families of gentile art lovers.

Lacemaking till wedded
betrothals and engagements
for those south of the river
refined for ladies at home,
cultivated by nuns for the poorest of flocks
artists gently framed
faded in a passage above
hidden photo renowned still for its age
forgotten elsewhere, swift nimble fingers
in streets where one income and trade
is exchanged for another
mirroring sisters, the French quarter now silent.

Cork arts foyer

She sniffs the acrid sour smell of the poetry magazine
Lying on the rear side table, piles scattered around
Young, plump, beautiful
In an old-fashioned way
Preoccupied with a previous call
Her excuse for not speaking.

Deep greys and ochres behind publication lines
Large, looked down on by poster-lined walls
Some curled ends like the locks of the girl
Each telling stories of old writers, new actors
Now papering walls
On a cold winter's night.

Gazing down on the cliques, pairs, and loners
Waiting to enter dazed, expecting familiar
Disappointed, remembering youth
When the world was possible
Caught up in the act again, captured in beauty
Spoken words in newspapers, competition success.

Slim published volumes or old yellowed
Sheets lying between them
Unexpected delights
Merely a word unsaid at the right moment
That phrase or glance
On a cold winter's night.

To Seamus Heaney

In the heart of the season for blackberries
Gathering them every day in the forest on the hill
Above the house which never felt home,
Where I oozed in the luxury of blackberries
In a kitchen, watching and feeling them juicing
Within the hour after reaching the entrance
To the path
Allowing freedom
Invisibility.

In the heart of the season for blackberries
Writing seems inevitable from the bowels of my room
Below, looking up to the pathway lit by candles
On the last night of the year, every year since
Coming and dreaming of fruit from the forest
After the late spring and cold winter
Blueberries, strawberries, and blackberries
Randomly hiding.

In the heart of the season for blackberries
Recalling your writing, your departure
After I had written finding your poem
Your voice in the story of gathering the fruit
Dripping and soaking, the collection remaining
Beyond your journey leading us further
Into the heart of the forest and field
Gathering blackberries.

Blackberry summer chutney

> *500 grams of summer's fat blackberries*
> *140 grams of fine caster sugar*
> *140 grams of rich red onions sliced*
> *3 tablespoons of chopped fresh root ginger*
> *2 tablespoons of mustard, Dijon is best*
> *150 mls of white wine vinegar*

Combine ingredients, except for your vinegared wine,
use a saucepan large enough to take
mixing over medium heat,
just enough till your blackberries burst
dripping, oozing
as Seamus Heaney wrote,

> *At first, just one, a glossy purple clot*
> *Among others, red, green, hard as a knot.*
> *You ate that first one and its flesh was sweet*
> *Like thickened wine: summer's blood was in it*
> *Leaving stains upon the tongue and lust for picking.*

Then back to this moment,
season the magic liquid
with salt and pepper to taste,
add vinegar
just a touch at first,
lick for the senses
savour, then add all and allow
to simmer, uncovered
like the gentlest of brews
for just on ten minutes.

    Breathe in deeply
    enjoy the fragrance and bouquet,
    now pour your rich purple juice
    in a simple glass vessel,
    an everyday jar will do
    pure, sterilised if this be your way
then seal at once
to lock in the flavour
aroma, and pure joy of the moment.

Bank holiday in Ireland

Seems very British
bank holiday in Ireland
memories of Eliot, T.S.
yellow and dark
sitting in black
on leather
dark brown
cracked with years of silent wear
and gin
on bank holidays.

Dublin bus strike

Gold bus pulls up at Patrick's quay
responding
to tickets booked online
for expectant backpackers
reserving flights
going out.

Bus drivers united
no regular lines
travelling down or across
returning up north
as the strike up in
Dublin moves into day two.

A serious business
in economic crisis
all mutter and nod in sympathy
on the quay
then agitated stumble
and mumble in protest.

Got to get back!
They assured us they'd run
bank holiday or not
all secure
but no accounting for the fact
that bus drivers would be out.

A strike for what's rightfully theirs
while passengers agitate
aroused at the thought
that a Dublin strike
might leave them all
stranded.

Grand silence

A regular choice, still closed
just past dark
crate of empties waits at the front
7.10 it opens, a sign says 7.00
stools without welcome
perched still on tables,
outside white plastic chairs
soon smoked by frequent trucks
rattling in early morning rush.
>Sign above the door
>mirrors tiled across a far wall
>memories flash, north Africa
>touch of class where once
>the pet shop stood
>with kittens begging, hoping
>pedestrians gazing in
>would understand their misery,
>these captives
>behind grey glass.

Eyes glazed reflect restless hours
early morning risers fogged
from last night's spirits
dimming loneliness,
today's street
promising
friendliness, comfort
for those trapped
outside the silence.

Day transforming noisy street
darkly muted in the night
until crowds mingling
chance kind greeting
meets early morning
after silence
forgotten in the newest
dawning of light.

Searching trees

Two grey men silent as wood
the colour of old newspaper
glasses dulled by dim electric light
look up offended
holding the speaker, stranger
an intruder at bay,
annoyed at disturbance
to local research in Cork.

Private realm for the committed
sacred for those dedicated
belonging and owning
a heritage worth asking
for sharing and claiming
but not for others
foreign faced outsiders and outcastes
desiring respectability.

A legacy of Irishness
birthright of Corkness
of belonging to the honest
unknowing gentry,
so look of relief when the question
is of shipwrecks
Cork harbour 1830s and 40s
not transportation, marriage, or migration
people abandoning, defeated
dismissed, disregarded.

A valid local question here,
coastline shipwrecks fair
where grey men drift back to dull seas
of newspapers aged and damp
musty and faded where print blurs
a past most choose to forget.

Endangered species

Cork trees don't grow in Ireland
any more than rubber or bananas
but this is how it was known
to those who could not speak
the language of great grandmothers
more than a century and a half ago.

Corcaigh they said and might have spelt it
though other ears heard something close
to Cork, and so it became
stories and songs from this southern beauty
lasting long in family's line
sprouting from trunks grown so tough.

Trees on the Tipperary side here too
and Dublin's tales and of Kildare
delving and digging for scattered seeds
no easy task in history's garden
searching beyond names in dull, faded records
exploring in yarns still passed down.

The 237

Checking timetables for later
and later buses to the west
crying out purpose
reincarnation, spirits calling
sun glimmering on flagstones
golden brown florals
triangles, tri leaves
        and trinities on this first day
        at Imbolc.

Spring openly calling
hourly buses
rain sourly hanging round
like the bearded man on the pavement
cap held before him
hoping for a coin
to cover a shot of whatever,
        caffeine for remembering
        whisky to forget.

Buses arriving predictably
on the hour by the bridge
empty for those with minds too full
to remember
that spring is so near.

Rendezvous

Studs up the back of boots
lined with white fleece
greet sneakers still white in the rain
step forward as he backs back
push him closer to the red sign
stopping cars taking shortcuts through the lane.

Black plaits tied back
jeans tight screaming reverse
as he retreats
woollen-capped brimmed for sun
to cover red eyes burning from late nights
baggy jeans respectable.

Foil hides a roll filled with meat
as she stalks off with a small package
of powder she tests, dust silver wrapped
while moss in the corner
beneath the red sign
lies silently, listening.

Alone, without repeating
words shared, debated, eyes pleading
on the corner
beneath the red sign
silently demanding
– stop.

Poster at the station

Heads wanted – shaved and dyed,
nearby a body sleeping on a bench
head bowed low, unaware
of the red spotted graze on his skull
right at the end,
heading outward
to better places
home from the city where no one belongs
headlong into the danger of greyness
with cash from a social security cheque.

Head over heels with the girl down the road
or the lad at the garage her sole hope
heads full of dreams of belonging
or loneliness and forgetting
heads wanted, head chefs
head of something or other
heading nowhere important
no longer urgent but needed,
empty head, dreamer
heads wanted
for shaving, dyeing
craving altered with change.

Food for the dreamer

Saturday night fish and chips
seem rather mundane
ordinary for all who come out in the rain
away from the sea to a place inland,
tradition known well
fish and chips on the weekend
bring small comfort
to secret desire and fantasy hidden
from summer lodgers yearning *spaetzle*.

Delight in flat chips matched with sea catch
while seamen and coast people complain
it's not as it used to be
so little to claim,
small delight on a wet weekend night
for truly no exchange for the chips
salty and hot
thick, juicy
dream bites of youth.

Labyrinth

Through many hidden passageways
down narrow shaded lanes
history's forgotten stories lay
waiting for sunshine in the labyrinth.
> Behind buildings' dark coated walls
> waiting to be asked again
> who sang their songs and whistled tunes
> raised spirits through this labyrinth.

Along the path wait speckled doves
sparrows and lost seagulls' mates,
lunch time revellers leaving gifts
on tables down the labyrinth.
> Out into sunshine, out across the road
> into another maze of lanes
> each special personality matching
> graffitied art on canvas walls.

Again at night in new dress donned
lamps lit as they have been
long before the trend set in
to bring them back where deals were done.
> Winding down and through a maze
> lost chapters from the past
> exciting if we knew the tales
> lone voices through the labyrinth.

Gone are weeds which grew in cracks
along the brick ramparts
where on the flagstones underneath
late footsteps trudge their weariness.

    Above the same blue gazing down
    with love's own cheerful blanketing
    stark summer sun, umbrellas spread
    bold colours cheer the laneways.

Beneath the awnings rain pours down
on summer's late September day
protection under stars at night
for those who hear them yarning on.

    Musicians gather there to sing
    the tunes they've always sung
    when life is quiet, and lights go out
    in history's humming labyrinths.

An Bhrid – River Bride

– a river in counties Cork and Waterford, it is a tributary of the Munster Blackwater. Rising in the Nagle Mountains, it flows eastward, passing through the towns of Rathcormac, Castlelyons, Conna and Tallow, before joining the Blackwater at Camphire, 4.8 kilometres north of Youghal. The poet Edmund Spenser is reputed to have written part of his poem 'The Faerie Queene' on the banks of the Bride in the Conna area.

> dancing river bride
> delights twisting and bending
> welcoming arms wide

The Bride from the Lee

Eight otters live at Blackpool
where erection of the shopping centre
passageway channels a narrow leafy
arm of the Lee,
River Bride gliding
underground to dark and hidden drains
where peaceful waters
flow locked away
beyond the reach of birds who know it well
swooping down to fish
or watching clouds float by
reflected with the sun on happy days.

Now the dirge 'there goes the Bride'
is sung with mournful tunes, another fable made
passes down with others, lost tradition
until one day, years ahead, a history buff will search
the tale of how once cheerful otters swam and dove
and fished the waters near a bridge
at Blackpool, where pools no longer pause
where none remember days
when youngsters swam and old men fished
where women gathered yarning.

Brigid's track

'Bavaria beer' written bold on the back
and right along the side of a truck
travelling north on the route,
signs on the road recall nuns of our youth
dressed in the black
they carried from Eire
Port Laois, Abbeyleix
Carlow with Tullow
and on to Kildare.

No blue signs on a freeway
when Brigid travelled this way,
Mary of the Gael the old ones called her
woman of legend no patron of the road
for those who know the signs
trucks and campervans
reading highway boards
a history known to few.

Brigid's women
largely faded in the past
few remain in civil dress
old women like the rest
still gazing at the stars
still hoping for the signs again
steering to better times.

Lost story

Did you reach these shores
I want to ask you now
For I found your life
Hidden deep inside
In a wooden box
Only archives knew
Standing silent long
After all had gone.

Did you send your words
With sailing monks
On their way with news
To far away folk
With their old stories
Of trees and sacred things
Frozen hard in tales.

Could you ever guess
They would keep your tale
In a state library
In a country far
That I'd read online
Of a long-lost text
That Cogitosus
Wrote in year six hundred.

Did you write new songs
Tunes which sang of love
Speaking not of fear
Nor the curse sent down
Only kindest words
For the faithful crowds
Who heard parables
He'd told long ago.

Otter on the Bride

There's an otter the man's seen
On the Bride
Foxes, badgers, stoats, and mink,
And he's captured on film
Heron, wagtails, mallards
And a kingfisher near dippers
Amazing little birds to watch
Flipping stones, using Bride's currents
Where they walk under water
Searching for small gems.

It's alive he proclaims
Of this old water
Which appears claimed by waste
Flowing down to Cork's urban waterway,
Undervalued, misunderstood
Where the city's planners want to hide
What they claim is an eyesore
Without venturing and pondering
As he has, observing freshwater shrimp
Hearing birds among reeds.

No open drain this river flowing
Alive through the floods,
Tidal barrier from the wetlands
Home to the fish and otters
Who dive hopefully
For their sole source of food,
I want my children
To grow up Chris says smiling
Moody with the river
And the otters who live by it.

By rivers

Did she ever weave with rushes
a carpet or sign to hang beside
the fireplace, or above the door
leading from snow
and cold outside,
the symbol travelling
across seas
which still few remember
beyond knowing it had
some special meaning,

a song
to mark another new spring
day they still call
Imbolc.

Snowdrops

Snowdrops at Imbolc
arrive with season's switching
recollecting Bride
dressed in cloak of cream
        woven to match first snowdrops
        past winter solstice
        spring equinox promises
        bursting through late snow.

Sonnet for a storm

Unfair to call it Brigid's gale this year
Her name known more for kinder gifts to folk
A past now fading dim on mornings clear
Far back with myths our history invokes.

These stories frailer than the new spring storm
The wild destructive rains of Brigid's day
On coastal towns where rushing waters form
Grey torrents sweeping all which calmly lay.

She makes her mark this spring reminding all
Of ages past, a history living still
Of hearths secured and harvests standing tall
When spirits soared, folk stood formidable.

As wild winds lash the stormy shores ahead
We see clouds part on peaceful paths we tread.

New dreaming

We were few among the many
who could tell of Brigid's ways
the name of the woman now long past
hardly heard of now at baptismal fonts
for a generation or two
few Bridgets.

A name common in towns
where Irish farmed land
marched for St Patrick's day
composed songs remembering Brigid
schools set up evoking cells
fading gently in a new century's phase.

The spirit of dreaming
has taken on new depths
on an island continent open to hear it
beckoning again
to hear voices of the land
our pioneer stories considered anew.

Family stories thought afresh
retold and passed on down
understood from a new perspective
ancient tales blend in a different way
different spirit of the land
new basis of learning.

Light through the window

Wondering how you knew, I saw
the light shining through the window,
it showed weaving bold and clear
rushes pretending gold reflected,
right over left, down across the other
branched back again.

Forming the ancient symbol,
sign I thought only we knew
then realised this was yours,
your sign, and I the stranger
you the one for whom the meaning
reflected life, your heritage
our symbol only
because they carried it afar.

Hanging at the entrance
Brigid bless wherein we dwell
every fireplace, hearth, and kin,
and I thought of childhood kitchens
with it hanging at the doorway
as Jewish neighbours hang a sign
to mark their own place
and stories of freedom.

Few know our cross from rushes carried far
formed right over left and back again,
you hung it shining
gold with purple light through hazy gauze
and I saw it through your window
reflected on my screen.

Searching for Bride

The strange thing about never having been there
is that some believe you never were,
others see you everywhere around home
men and women of yesteryear
those newly searching imbued
with your story saved in plaster and stone
standing outside chapels for believers
with forebears who sailed across seas.

No strange thing for the people of land, lochs
and fountains, trees pointing the way
along a trail where you walked
routes where those traipsing the countries
nearby, took your story still found in books
now locked away in secreted archives
permission and ID needed for access
relics in their own way, even if not yours.

All the time lasting in myths of that past time
where those with new messages had silently placed
you, woman who might have held hands with
other wise ones, goddesses of fog's history
which none can remember or care
sentiment aside, it was time when the leaders
and wisest were women, the Meabh and the Brighid
those ones walking the hills, hallowed
found in manuscripts beyond wild crashing seas.

Sign to Kildare

A brown sign announces County Kildare
billboards profane announce sex
radio, ice creams
unconnected but side by side
seirbhisi shows services coming up
if the bus pulls over,

but it fails to stop
deadlines to meet
so blue signs stream past
flashes in the night
as the bus chortles
on its way back to Dublin.

Fifty-seven more
like apostles on the way
or was it fifty-two
along a freeway full, both double lines
though the bus runs alone
on this day of strike.

Another brown sign shows Kildare
Cill Dara, place of Brigid
but no visit today
to abbey or wells
nor to the square with a pub
named brazenly the Vatican,

to the town where a grandfather great
was once born
more than a century and a half ago
the town he revisited once more
the one lost in time's annals,
lost as today's bus travels on.

Question

Do you know Kilvurra?
She shakes her head
from Midleton
sitting here in another frontier land.

Few do but I found it
on a map
surrounded by green swathes,
I wrote a poem on it
and she looks at me strangely
too many memories
so far away
from a town where she lived to the east.

Near Bride's abbey

The nuns came each day from Kilbreda on the train
We would greet them with glee if earlier we arrived,
Tess and Ivan schooled their twelve girls there
But our mother said they were ladies, long before
Mumbling about the school too rich and expensive for us
Though I knew the Smiths had so little to spare.

Thinking back now there were shadows and darkness
Black habited discipline, sun's rays shining through,
There were kind women among them
Anselm and Stephen, and the Moira we loved
The one whose father owned the racehorse he trained
Recalling The Dip winning the '59 Melbourne Cup.

There was a spirit among them
Taken for granted strength learnt
In the wide new brown land,
Proud if I dared tell them we too were
Of Kildare, and I'd sing of the grandfather
Near Bride's abbey, who instilled the same in us
A sign we were from there, nobility or not
Grand, bound in the spirit of her place.

Bulldozed convent

Kildara is no longer standing
on the corner of Malvern's high street
home of past college for young trainee teachers
a school, and mother house for nuns.

A convent bull-dozed mid the sighs
and wailing of spirits long past
one sign of Brigid's women now gone
reduced by the changes of time.

Levelling grand houses of nuns long past
to rubble, too expensive to maintain,
dreams lost in machinery's invasion
living on still in stories we tell.

Cells of remembering an Ireland long past
faith spread by a Dara, Breda, and Bride
Brigid a new Esther, Mary of the Gael
unknown to pedestrians traipsing High Street.

An Abhainn Mhór – River Blackwater

– a river known in Irish as the Big River, flows through counties Kerry, Cork, and Waterford. It rises in the Mullaghareirk Mountains in County Kerry and flows easterly through County Cork, on through Mallow and Fermoy, then enters County Waterford, flowing on through Lismore before abruptly turning south at Cappoquin, where it drains into the Celtic Sea at Youghal Harbour.

> grand rivers tell tales
> recalling lives along banks
> coupling with love song

Where the Bride meets the Blackwater

Fresh stream stretches of Blackwater
and the Bride which weaves into it,
another salmon river with its havens
of pools, streams, and glides
their good push of water coming through
spring fishing at Fermoy and Careysville,
Ballymacpatrick in the old days
with fish just the same.

The Bride, upstream of Fermoy
with tributaries blessed for grilse fishing
those returning for the first time
as I do today,

>   no connection with the number of sea winters
>   for it's spring when we count them.

And here where the Bride bows gracefully
to the Blackwater's call
are the mammals, pine marten
and badger, Irish hare, and Natterer's,
Daubenton's and whiskered bats
the brown long-eared and pipistrelle

>   all feeding along the river,
>   roosting under bridges
>   and in old buildings.

Perhaps you've seen them
with the rudely named common frog
and the rare so much treasured
bush cricket, and the warbler
        seen in reeds and willows along the river
          embankments on the Blackwater and Bride.

The Blackwater

Dull name for the river gurgling downstream
Belching in spring's early downpour
Flooding, recrossing Fermoy's diversion
By-passing accidents with rolled trucks on highways
On this day of the furies before Valentine's feast,
>   Blackwater's key to the stories back and forth
>   Into Youghal homes, fields, and farms
>   And on to big houses once proud along the river
>   Where family names were passed down
Before fading with each new generation.

No longer recognised as barges and boats
Are few along its course, today's flooding
Forbidding old ways, futile endeavours
As highways and freeways transport goods too heavy
To withstand the fury of the storm
>   Just as moored ships in Cork's harbour
>   Were tossed wrecked on the coast, unnamed
>   Or too many to be worth reporting in daily press
>   Passed down by children transporting them
Further than trucks, never to return.

Dreaming and telling stories of Youghal
And places they dreamt of seeing along the river
Yearning again to smell spring soil lying sweet
And summer coastline days
Where shore's coarse emotions reflected in people
>   Life's seasons, forgotten
>   Except for those visiting places with stories
>   Old newspapers, musty archives with thin books
>   In libraries which tell stories of the Blackwater,
Those dreams which sank beyond its silent flow.

Thistledown

Fairies sang your name my child
Deep and sweet through forests
Lost in time's forgetfulness.

Unspoken name
No photographs taken
While spirits of deep green valleys
Clasped your hand.
For you became one with them
Learning their songs, enticing.

Fairies calling in the morning
With birdsong hardly awake
In the shadows.

Still moving with moods glimpsed
Only by life in the deep forest,
Squirrels, field mice
Snakes and lizards
With other folk never seen
In the harsh daylight of our living.

You, fairy child
Captured
In raptures with their singing.

Pilgrimage

Rite of passage means more
than pilgrimage
but like flowers and wild herbs gathered
for magic and dreams
words take on new interpretations
for the song.

Each year another journey to the place
where old women trod
as wee girls knowing little
beyond villages and their loves,
like wildflowers and forest birds
following nature's bedding ways.

Pilgrimage to places no longer on maps
baptisms in old registers
and blessing near wells,
stones forgotten by ordnance books
love for daughters where stone rings lie still
in green of fields at the end of a road.

Midleton

You tell me the story of your grandfather
I tell you of mine
and our lives are entwined
shaped by the place we find ourselves
inhabiting today
shaped by the reputation we have
our grandfathers had.

Others far away tell their own stories
so their grandfathers are seen as noble
shining or suffering
in an honourable cause
we all tell the tales and events
our own way
each with its truth
defining where we stand
on the edge of the carpet.

That faerie queen

You gave me music for the words I wrote
Long before I knew of your existence
Before I knew the story which we told
Was shared by both across years and distance.

Your sister too recorded on the harp
Perhaps the very harp which she once played
By chance the family music handed down
With names you salvaged, poetry remade

To suit a modern time's romantic tales
Until we came with family questioning
Who was the woman hailed in Tara's Halls?
Whose legacy remained in melody.

Then came the stories from east of Cork
Another *faerie queen* we hardly knew.

In Tara's halls

The woman in the photograph
dressed in cuffs of lace
looks across the centuries
with eyes which speak of grace.

Ribbons from the bonnet
hang down beside the face
stray hairs escape to form a frame
to show her fine good taste.

She looks out calmly, hints a smile
the years have formed her strong
she sold the lace and ribbons fair
while her children she loved long.

She sings the songs of long ago
remembering all their tunes
she passes on the music
as peaceful life resumes.

She senses life is struggle too
but she's known a gentler past
decency and fine things
she teaches these will last.

The woman in the photograph
is remarkable it's true
she came upon the Earl Grey 2
when privileges were few.

She lived in Youghal and then Ardmore
when still she was a lass
she made her home in Campbell Town
with her haberdashery shop.

Many children she did have
raising them best she could
first with John and Jabez next
they turned out rather good.

Born a Walsh her good self was
though from Erin's Isle she came,
there lived her life and loved all well
faced heartache with a smile.

Descendants now can tell the tales
of music, trade, and farms
all brought up strong they did their best
used wit and strength and charm.

The woman in the photograph
is grandmother to us all
in memory great or two times great
this little woman now stands tall.

Where rushes grow

Creeks at home sound different
from rivers, brooks, and springs of younger lands,
our billabongs rest silently, patiently
until discovered
by one unwary
no intention more than wandering
aimlessly
until there is no energy left
no rippling, gurgling, bubbling
chocked between the boulders
blocking waterfalls with their moss
       white fairies skipping over rocks.

There are no hermitages at home
no carved cells of saints or monks of old
though paintings in the wildest parts calmly
tell their stories
of the spirit
for those travelling songlines
assured
that these protect and show the way
for hunting, singing, dancing,
their catch prepared in fires
on lands unhindered by voices
       of fairies on white water.

Declan's well

Just past the feast of Declan
old sister telling her rosary stopped,
an Irish colleen with lovely red hair
she said,
I told her of the woman a century ago
oh one of the Walshes from just out here
as if she knew her,
maybe born in Youghal
though lived round here for sure
you're probably a cousin of mine
she said.

All the while an old man did the rounds
of the well and the church
and the graveyard beyond,
an Our Father and Hail Mary
the sign into the enclave
read.

A Russian drank water from the well,
I thought of other oceans in between
isolation, acceptance
belonging to this place
with only the sound of seagulls
and lapping of waves below.

Ardmore

At the end of five-mile walk round the cliffs,
past Declan's well
and back into town
past a cottage right on the street
an old man stood
looked at me
and said
>*you never know who ye'll see*
>*walking down the street*

with strong Ardmore accent.
I laughed
and so did he.

Presence

Sensing her more here than in Youghal
feeling her near
on this warm summer's day
on the cliff-walk path above Ardmore
    while the battery at my ear
    blips three once more
    finished
still, other sounds here
sing to me
full concentration
in tune

Frigate

Calm shadowed birds on the wall of my room,
> in worn gnarled trees
> along the road
> fluttering on bare branches
> touching the window,

gentle doves
snow white
against the soft, blinding azure
of the sea
fluttering even at night.

This seems the season
> for earth's creatures
> in love

but not for me
this pull
to a deeper gravity
and call, yearning
not this time to move on,
> a call which drives the white
> frigates near the lighthouse.

The Helen

We could have been Canadian
If only for the gale
The storm which broke the ship apart
When all their struggles failed.

The brothers Walsh all shipmen were
Owners of *The Helen* proud
They worked her well with cargo too
Crossed seas when winds allowed.

It roared and swept the harbour long
Now written in the annals
All was lost at sea that night
No safety in Cork's channels.

Livelihood of all their kin
With father once a seaman knew
They faced the truth in '46
Their future prospects few.

Their ship was gone and all aboard
No more an ocean link
So new horizons now they sought
New Brunswick past the brink.

Three seamen James, Will and brother John
With sisters and their elders went
Leaving Mary Ellen home
Her guarantee for finance lent.

Companion for her Bransfield aunt
Distressed to see all go
They'd joined the queue with Irish clans
Dreams waning high and low.

On to St John's at New Brunswick
Great port for seamen's stories
They worked their skills with other ships
Though failed returning glories.

Once grand owners of their ship
She, the one the gale destroyed
Compete they tried but found it hard
Walsh bankbooks soon were void.

With two onto Nevada gone
To search the silver mines
These seamen's hearts in deserts dried
Still dreaming coastal climes.

Walsh stories long they went to tell
As they married Irish maids
Lived their lives in northern lands
But Ireland did not fade.

Their youngest sister back at home
To another south land went
Beyond her dreams when all she longed
Were kin but distant funds were spent.

Many stories and seamen's tales
Are lost and hidden far away
Still some tell of Walshes brave
Their dreams in past gone days.

At the clock tower

At a pub in town
where there was a sign last night
>*join Mick Walsh for a singalong*
>*in the back room*

there were a couple of young sandy type of men
lounging on the outside door
whenever I passed,
there again today
with others
just congregating
chatting
recollections of a marketplace
for lounging hardly seems the word
to use for rendezvous.

Youghal lighthouse

She told me yesterday that it would be a fine day
that showers would not come till evening
      then predicted that today
      would be raining,
her father and her boyfriend were both boat men
they always checked these things,

but I walked
forgetting
fascinated
along the path beside the lighthouse
sensing danger
on these rocks above the sea
      trodden by sailors and pirates
      for centuries
      while silent nuns nurtured the flame
      in the coast's lonely beacon.

Old photos

Scattered and yellowing,
Mellowing sepia the fashion or faded grey from years
Of neglect, carelessness and forgotten memories,
Photos searched through when the whole generation
Has gone, has passed away or as the Greeks say passed on,
Scattered lives timeless in photos now.

Little boy frowning at a camera,
Dressed in sailor suit and boater no wonder,
The young lad later so proud of his infantry uniform
The only thing for a boy from the bush
Conscripted not volunteering,
'It'll be a long war' his father warned.

Scattered years no camera records
Though perhaps in a drawer or box long forgotten
No photos for the boy in the bush
With the father who rabbited and fished or did unnamed things,
The Depression with a capital
Which depressed and repressed and refused youth their lives.

The boy on the milk cart smiling with pride,
The man's hat, man's coat poking fun at the child,
The horse's head hanging, depression forgotten in youth's fun
Skilled as those men were in survival
And making do, the boy never speaks of years missed,
Life in the schoolyard, the classroom, and work.

Stories of nuns and Irish schoolmarms,
'Old Spuds we called her' as she stands at the back frozen
In a rare class photo in a room with long desks, benches, and smiles
At the Sacred Heart school in Yarrawonga,
We went through those faces, our dad and I
When the photo turned up through an old school friend.

He's dead. He's gone, he's gone. He's still lingering on.

Only four of the boys now men remembering, and alive,
The McPhersons, the Quinns, the Walshes and Ryans,
The new breed of Joneses and Johnsons, Jessops and more
Photos of a three-year old, boy in grade three, then working lad
Youngster in uniform, a boy with his mates.

Posing for a photo for the mantelpiece at home,
Fox Studios gives us regalia rough and still silky skin
The private A class who he jokes leaves B class
The man without shirt, arms round his mates,
Mates on the beach under palm trees at Rabaul
A New Guinea we know before married to neighbour.

Like bullets from their rifles while they
Unprepared unsuspecting struggle through,
We now flip through photos and we throw into heaps
A moment in history,
The boy born in a Depression now frozen as memory
Years still to pass and generations to come.

We glance and move on uncaring for thoughts,
The people their sadness, their loves and dreams
Generalities of the past save the expected salute,
Over and gone now
Lost in concerns of new depressions, again recessions,
Our yesterdays on film, the future their tribute.

Connectivity

You're not connected to a network
the screen says over and over again
through ancestry's network
both sides of Cork connected across years
with clouds and seas between
lost stories old pieced anew
to make pictures clear.

A scene through rained-speckled glass
window cold without vague
blurred then opening clear again,
it takes only a twist from down to up, then wide
to a new dimension, an old burial ground
few named, waiting, expecting.

Connectivity unknown to most
making stories to fill gaps of wondering
like history's travellers
unconnected, out of place
out of time, spirits wandering seeking
open hearts reconnecting.

Abhainn na Bandan – River Bandon

– The Bandon (from ban-dea, meaning 'goddess') rises in Maughanaclea Hills in West Cork, flows east and eventually southeast to Dunmanway, turns eastward then flows in a broad fertile valley with woodlands, through the centre of Bandon town, eventually ending at Kinsale where it drains into the harbour on the Irish south coast. The river is crossed by fifteen bridges (including two footbridges), and had four railway bridges, one still intact on farmland near Dunmanway.

> your sleeping beauty
> winding through woodland valleys
> upholding nature

Climbing trees

From childhood, a large tree stood majestic
Pussy willow outside the kitchen window
Above a wood heap where the old man
Dealt with startled ducks or chickens
Each year a day before December's meal.

The greatest feature coming of age at ten
Was to climb it high and far
Out to the second highest branch
Where none had further ventured
Over the creek where rushes grew.

Beyond that year there were no more
Grand trees for climbing brave again
A new house on bare, grassy paddocks
Waving in breeze alongside the railway line
Where trains dropped coal, secret and warm.

Climbing Irish trees old roots were saved
Other lands filled in distant branches
Enough to hold though rarely more
Than that furthest branch none too far back
The one we dreamt to climb beyond.

The bride at Broken Creek

She rests in Victoria's Shepparton
Thinks no more of Shepperton Lakes
Far away near Skibbereen
With its lake still stocked with trout.

The name gave some comfort
Far away from the place of her birth
Broken Creek called home now
The grey river reflecting a relocated heart.

Ngurai-illam-wurrung before they called it broken
Deep pond lagoon near a new Shepparton
Land stark and dry, far from mossed forests
Of the home she still saw in her dreams.

How often did she stare out wide?
Brown river nagging each day
Dreaming of the green black lakes
Near the place they renamed Shepperton.

Not called this in her tongue, a language they stole
Hounded out when they called it another
Not Shepperton Lakes long ago in the mist
But another now long forgotten.

Lough Skahanagh before they named it Shreelane
Sheltered lakes calling fishermen,
With its cousin Lough Hyne calling ducks
Breeding, before renaming it Shepperton.

Her heart half broken in floods, new river land
Green turned to brown then black with summer fire,
Another land far from green, black glistening lake
West Cork heartache settles silent in far dusk.

Finding Coill Mhura

'Tis up very high
The men in Dunmanway tell me
Up so very high, they say thrice more,
Left to wonder if a warning
Too high to reach
Beyond clouds
This place called Kilvurra
Coill Mhura, woods of a saint
Sacred or not, shrine perhaps
Hidden high on the hill
Beyond searching.

Climbing up and around towards
Grey windmills looking about
To engulf me
Proclaiming to own me
Up there on the hill
Among others standing high Alone
Around a turn towards silver
Sentinels with arms opened wide
Halting rather than welcoming
Embrace.

Who goes there?
I hear them demanding
Who comes on this hill?
And to whose do you come
Here on this road
Which way to turn
At the end
Called Kilvurry
the GPS seems to say
Turn right
Then take Kilvurry all the way.

There at the end sure enough is a wood
A black forest looking back
Leading right to the top,
I wish I had stayed away
From the fir trees together thick enough
To paint a grove dark
Listening,
Believing these are kin
This their place long deserted
Dwelling overgrown.

Overgrown beyond the gate standing open,
Machine long abandoned
Locked away for the day
On this Sunday of rest.
Hay bales covered in plastic
Black out of place, matched only by the wood
In mystery's place
Way up here at the entry
To Mhura's dark wood.
Under pines and firs now like night.

Red road fuchsia-lined
Blinking in profusion
Standing
Waving the way
Crowds cheering
I've come to the ground
The place where the farmer said
I must place my feet,
Black and white flag
Flashes on the screen
Announcing the place.

My arrival
To the place they called Qoill Mhura.
As the ark finally rests
Near a clearing at the top of the hill
Where a clear summit light
Opens to green all around,
To an old house on the left
Long since made new
Though the roof tells
Another story.

Lichen still claiming the place
where Donovans dwelt
There, where the fuchsias and fir trees end
Gazing down on gold and green
Spread all round, far below
That moment at the end of the path
Where the road peters out
Two single tracks, no more,
Enough room for a cart or a car
No other passing the opposite way.

From Mhura's fir trees, strong arms
Where entrance claims
No exit
Allows no intruders to leave,
Claims those who dare or care enough
Holding them firm
Broken-hearted
That its children and beloved have left
Far across seas where fuchsias did not bloom
In such profusion with the gorse
Along dark roads
To a wood named for yearning.

At the end of a side road

Standing there and clearly marked
at the end of the dead-end road
        grey winding from the yellow routes
half-forgotten by any save locals
wanting shorter ways round homelands,
almost invisible in the orange of highways
        and serrated grey and white of the national route
dotted line from an unfinished road to Kilvurra.

No signs pointing to the town where long before
families lived, were born, and baptised
        their records no longer warrant note, invisible
GPS but a point near the mound on google earth
there in the green surrounds of old faiths
deserving a name for those caring to find
        a place where for centuries communities gathered
at Mass Stones, stories remembered, understood.

Surrounded by stones standing still
near burial grounds marked on the crest of the mound
believing and praying to a god we know not who
        cycles of life and death feeding this ground
Kilvurra a cell in the woods, meaning
forgotten in time as languages moved on
        missing the stories of lives since long gone
where death meant not end but land's renewal.

At the end of a side road on a map all in green
Kilvurra stand humbly to attention
still significant enough to appear
        on a map though others are all lost now in time
migrations, enclosure, lost lands, starvation
records becoming reference points across seas
        where new names replace those now forgotten
        at this place near road's end on the map.

Kilvurra stones

Kept alive in records almost illegible
Inclined to be forgotten where greater roads loop
Linking today with the mystery of ageless vistas
Voices long gone call out for understanding
Unknown today their riches stories
Remembered in standing rocks and mass stones
Regal tall and upright to attention
Announcing still their spirit's kin and sacredness.

Bandon

Poacher's inn
Immaculata shrine
Peugeot showroom
on the edge of town,
        O'Donovan's restaurant
        with its rusted roof,
        reminding me of rural places
        far away in warmer climes,
        its wooden outhouses peeling paint
grey on winter's morning
lifted by the sun
near the old marketplace,
        tired painted sign
        boosting the main street plainness
        on the grudging river at the crossroads
Kebab house stands brightly open
for new wanderers waiting
for old children failing to return.

Bus stop

The loveliest place for a bus stop
a bench facing a road
where three streams intersect
a bench at the junction
on the midpoint between winter
and spring
facing new traffic and tales
with backdrop of water and stories
too old to remember.

Rock hard

water troughs scattered
like standing stones
memories of an ancient time
a land too old to remember
isolated on the landscape
alone
solitary

Storytelling

Searching far in Skibbereen
Sure this is where she's from
Then find Dunmanway parents signed her
In Kilvurra, a family Donovan.

It's only two greats further back
Which seems like yesterday
That Margaret stepped on southern land
Forever there to stay.

The *Eliza Caroline* shipped these girls
Pioneer skills we talk of now with pride
Their children and their kindred's own
All Aussies true and tried.

Names changed through generations
From Darebin, Kyneton, and Broken Creek,
Born near Skibbereen on a Dunmanway farm
The woman with that strong Irish streak.

Donovan was grand enough
In the land of Irish names
Yet glad we are whatever place
Her story still remains.

In a field

Pink soil freshly turned
mauve into purple
dull day grey sky
no reflection
colour of new pink-eyes
unexpected on a winter's day
moving into imbolc
faery tales and spirits stories
in the morning
on a blushing day.

Standing stones

Listen to the message on the wind
and catch sure signs in skies above
the hills where sun will filter through
this morning on year's longest day.

Where morning's grand silence
waits to be broken,
early sunrays stream to lands
it saw before days counting time.

Beyond deep forests cleared
on mountains high
where old light streams through
ancient stones stand still
        waiting.

For each new light announces
time touching dark places forgotten
through long winter's season
promised pilgrim messages
        renewed.

Here the spirit world remains
at peace on mountains gazing out
through valleys shrouded sombre still
on lakes where darkest depths hide
        secrets

Which only time knows waiting
for new summer light again,
for magic fires lit in late darkness
this splendid summer solstice night.

Solstice foraging

Now with dawn, deep silence gone
as crickets warm to birdsong
we forage for wild herbs as they did
long ago, to calm, to charm
to heal.

Oak leaf and wildflowers for crowns
wound with cornflowers,
chamomile and marigolds
sage, wild marjoram, and yarrow
for love

Then, by pathways collect elderberry
from deep in the forest far
away from lonely land sprayed toxic,
secret spots kept pure for drafts
enlivening.

Here crowned in first solstice sunlight
eyes sparkle, reflecting green ponds
rivers swollen in last melting snows,
restored in solstice gatherings
with song.

Listen to the message on the wind
and catch sure signs in skies above
grasslands and hills, where sun seeps
into year's longest day with messages
of possibility.

An Aighlinn – River Ilen

– a river in West Cork, rising at Mullaghmesha mountain (near Sheep's Head and St Finbarr's Way), it flows southwards for 34 kilometres into the Celtic Sea. It is listed as having quality water, making home for fish including brown and sea trout and Atlantic salmon. The river's main settlement is Skibbereen, before it flows into the sea at the village of Baltimore.

>in reeds near rivers
>warblers weave nests strung lightly
>from stems for new eggs

Ilen

Lights on the Ilen glimmering elongated
reflect soft streetlights
standing in place where they have been for years
along the road
where little traffic flows early.

No cats here arching fearful spines
fury reserved for farms
none seen in alleys or lolling about
in doorways
where old grey men stand waiting
or near windows
where bored young lads stand
pale so early.

Arches stare loudly as light beneath
along the west side reflect another
further along, and one more again
three mirroring three
on this third day of spring,
birds huddled away
in the grey of dawn
thinking it is winter,

while the line slowly lengthens
on the spot for the regular bus to Cork
where night moves slowly
into daylight
anticipating.

Sunday morning

Sunday morning Skibbereen
silent
Busy Bee at Hourihane's shuttered,
dark
Roycroft's rent-a-bike closed down now
has been for a year or three past
still others shut tight,

new ones open
freshly located Arts Centre looming
frowning down
gloomily
rebuking colours below

grey skeleton making some townsfolk
glad and proud
as eyes gaze up
away from the emptiness around

sign of the twenty-first century a local said
at Imbolc celebration a night or so back,
McCarthy and McGuire signs along the street
lanes without them frozen
naked

corner town-hall clock sadly strikes eleven
reminding the few faithful
that Mass will soon start

Sunday closed day for all till it's over
then O'Reilly's for coffee or tea
crossing the river
flowing out to the coast.

Friends

Friends drop in
sitting at the kitchen table while
a woman known along the street prepares late breakfast
for the old man who often drops by
after trudging dusty roads
and days spent rabbit hunting.

Always a kettle on the boil
some news or other or they make it up
only an hour or a half they say at the start
then up to the shops and again
on back home after it,
women courting company

Next door to Forge House

Surprise at the sight of a café
only pregnant in thought last year
where dreams over coffee
burst through,

old names forming
the backbone of a town
determined to thrive,

faces through windows
names written
in the register of life.

Dandelion down

White cat with red leather collar
        sits coiled and crouching
        in the thin green grass
        much like chives
        in front of the house
far behind on the hill.

Red windowpane and sills
        potted crimson geraniums
        mirror a reflection,
        five hours later the white cat lies
        asleep, foetal ball
        white dandelion down
fur hiding scarlet sleeping.

Reflecting rain

Raining over the roof of my world
drops bouncing on the flat roof
lying there, rotting slowly
demanding repair for the heart
beyond revamping.

Rain tolerating a sadness of the soul
surging unexpected from the heart
lying there waiting the release
allowing a spirit to be restored
unbreakable.

Raining in the thoughts of times
long before being and birthday
roaming the earth and finding one
willing to welcome spirits
desiring
one more chance.

Rain peacefully stroking the wood of the bridge
determined, this river
undisturbed by the heron
coming to fish every evening
near the bank
unthwarted.

Haiku on Skibbereen Bridge

on Skibbereen bridge
seagulls recall memories
never forgotten

linking land with land
bridging dreams with cold morning
life passing over

artists construction
artisans long labouring
lasting forever

Where otters greet the Ilen

They tell me the otters come to show
Themselves as gifts to Skibbereen
Right near the centre where we read
Of old times and people who were ours
People who saw the otters
As we do today.

Otters who make us smile
In the greyest morning's drizzle
Perhaps the forebears of the pair
Who came to fish today,
The otters in the Ilen river,
Creatures come to stay.

While further on we find them playing
Between the heron and the ducks
The mallard with six small chicks floating
Distracted by the jewelled kingfisher
Swooping down before the otter
Dives to claim her prize.

Sonnet at Mizen

To walk alone along the Mizen cliffs
Protected from the thrashing gale at sea
To watch the ships on calmer days in drifts
The life of dreams like cliff grass always free.

Its swaying cotton flowers bent with ease
Along the path which leads to rocks below
A ribbon floating in the morning breeze
It peters out the further down I go.

The gate now locked to keep trespassers out
Determined souls will always find ways through
Free spirits meant all customs here to flout
Those reclaimed stories told again anew.

For beauty ever draws the poet on
A vision for the artist never gone.

Woodland garden – Liss Ard

It was O'Donovan built this place,
Woodland garden where a grandmother keened
Unaware water bubbled into the well
From another deep near sky garden.

Sit on a bench in Skibbereen's woodland gardens
Green land to rest life-weary bodies and souls
Filled with greens multi-hued
Scented by blossom-lined fruit trees beyond.

Beyond mind's remembering now all is said
Told only by wind and birds calling above
The oak with remembrances ground in
Another life another century over and gone.

Gone are the people and the lives lived
Nightmares over, a new day beginning our dreams
Beginning this morning with new songs for singing
By all travellers who sit in woodland gardens.

At the poetry marathon

Was the woman who came in late
to the poetry marathon
the woman sitting opposite
at the reading
frowning
the same as the one I'd forgotten to ring
had missed days before
too late for the meeting
now
too late to create a story
or poem
about forgetting
about wanting to be alone
about space
and time
and aloneness
about wanting company
only
with the spirit
of the place.

After the hunger film

living
among shadows
patches of memory
remembering long ago,
all in the present
yesterday's memory
quelled
in today's rioting
future
uncertain.

Music at the corner pub

Monday's corner pub
musicians jam together
names changed, music blends
      moaning pipes alert
      fiddles to music making
      harmonies dancing
black beer harmony
bright softens gloomy spirits
lifting heaviness.

Wailing pipes cry out
bleak tearfulness forgotten
in joint harmonies
      joint music making
      old melodies remembered
      played in new ways
bagpipes raucous
moan in basso continuo
keeping all in accord

At Forge House

Today Joe's back in the guesthouse
old man with long white hair
wishing he'd been born
a hundred years ago because he can't stand
the traffic.

      I agree.

A French couple who appreciate broken French
her sister in Oz,
their daughter here somewhere
won't talk about themselves,
a Cork couple on bikes
both young, expectant
he reminds me of David
ex-Irish army Kabul.

Bells now tolling
join an overcast pale sky
one to remember as the owner mumbles
with guests it's 7-24-365,
and while they ring on
this memory's chime
delightful at breakfast,
there's another story to be told.

Convent for sale

Convent for sale on the crest of the hill
grey and imposing
frowning down on the street
rebuking the sign painted in red
for sale
just like a street woman selling her wares
the red sign selling
a convent in red
like lipstick spread thick
on a maid too young
bold and profane
in red, drawing a crowd
to the convent
for sale.

For rent

For rent sign on the dusty windows
which last year reflected
faces in glass shelves
contents weighing them down,
other windows freshly painted
new signs this month
like mascara on the girl
coming of age.

Festival windows

Poems in windows
blinking out to those vacantly passing by
pedestrian in their movements
enthralled in the latest gossip on corners
scratched away from the curb.

Indifferent with memory of yesterday's news,
complaining, explaining the meaninglessness
of what goes by the name of economy
finances of life destitute
reflection on life dictated.

Mirroring the commonplace
comfortable acceptance worth songs or verse
at least poems in windows waken new thoughts
calling them to retrace steps in time
back again, rereading, reflecting.

Autumn foraging

Wandering on another hill
hanging quiet above our town,
I wonder if they foraged as we do early
for autumn blackberries ripen quickly
with daytime warmth
seducing forest life
to forage on slow, cool days
when clouds hide sun
and early winter advent
threatens to choke and strangle life

Gathering forest blackberries
last wild juice spread in its heart
sweet raspberries from a field
without a name before them,
late strawberries transplanted,
porch box reminding as they finish
of the hope promising spring
next year one more renewal
after dead dark dreams.

Wondering about people
near darkened lochs of the west
if they foraged for berries as we do
relying on sweetness
sustaining when things were tough
adding change to life predictability,
heartbreak foreboding
land claimed, lives removed
captured for
that new place far beyond their shores.

Gathering berries

Did they gather blackberries
on that land across the sea?

Maybe they asked it as I question now
our uncertainties the same
for life without gathering blackberries
seems poorer and sadder.

Gathering blackberries
hearing them plop falling to the bucket
watching as they slowly turn to juice
mixed together before arriving home.

Purple dye from their washing
stains beneath fingernails
which day's passing fades.

Heated, transformed with more sugar
bubbling like the richest wine brews
blackberries life-giving for a moment or two.

Joy for the coldest late autumn afternoon
lasting through winter reminding us
of our delight
in gathering wild blackberries.

Sentinel

Sun out on the old railway bridge
seagull sentinel always there
when it shines
solitary
preening
with little to show
fluttering
casting off remaining raindrops
for early spring's warmth rarely lasts
chasing another
to the sea where
his mates fly.

This iron place is his
he'll not be moved
refusing to budge
from the place claimed
as his own
no waystation this bridge
only air traffic above
none crossing, disused now
claiming this as his place
guardian, sentinel
perched proud right on the midpoint
of the old railway bridge.

Reen Peninsula

Turn right from Union Hall
on the Skibbereen – Rosscarbery Road
and head south towards the sea
to the place where the artist
lives.

Alone for the moments of creation
then proclaiming
to the world a new child
stands ready
for consideration, acclaim
or puzzlement.

Here on the edge of an island
so far to the west of the world
to where it starts again
lives
in artist's dilemma
viewing, reviewing, reproducing
for critics' acclaim.

For Annie Sullivan

Australian artist Kelly
with no other place to rest
easel and canvas bound for wider landscapes
than with audience resting close to the sea
in the graveyard
where Annie Sullivan lay
by lapping edges where hedges divide
Rosscarbery from its neighbours.

This solitary artist from a south land
where others sailed a century and a half ago.

Spreading linen ready for the making
taking and breaking
virginal white
screaming attention, begging care
tearing fantasies only a lover can know
solid enough for a virginal bed
dry tombstone from a time long-ago
in those other lives wound into our story.

Now his muse and inspiration
her epitaph long after death.

Betty's apple

Back in Apple Betty's corner house
forgetting the strength of the caffeine fix
Java Republic the only solution
for a bitterness forgotten
in an air so sweet
flat white higher than the green hills
around on this Imbolc day
surrounded by organic sneezing
flying pollen takes no blame
mea culpa not for pollens
on this windiest day of new spring
still yearning for the wild sign of blossoms.

Back in Apple Betty's crossroad lounge
warm back shop mezzanine
Ballygowan water on the cool
for summer mornings dreams
music here tuned into folk
full rich warm bodied on the floor
whatever time of year
single swaying tree outside
sunblind edge flaps furiously in response
solitary reader immersed in morning's news
and others reminisce events with mild gossip
for all accepted here

all a sense of coming home.

Fire

Flames shimmer and dance through glass
Enticing the lonely with thoughts of love
Comforting a family with fires laid by children
While outside delight
Around a carefree campfire
Bush singing softly on warm autumn nights
Or in spring before summer
When far forest fire fears halt all.

In winter's cold houses
Chilblains, sadness and loneliness
Fill longing children
Parents out working for the next pay cheque
Somehow somewhere else to escape
Boredom and sameness, unable to ignore
Cold's cries and complaints
Antagonism brimming over.

Into childhood
Flames from the fire fanning fantasies
Of love, understanding, care
Belongingness past evening
When again grey ashes of morning
Are cleared by children
Or tired mothers
Worn out with beyond tomorrow.

Soup kitchen

Old soup kitchen with many lives
Stands expectantly
The red sign there another year
Moss and small grasses line highest levels
Windows boarded across horizontal
Spaces at the top to let a little light
Shine through for spirits
Roaming round.

Shuttered windows pass as doorways
Black with age look newly oiled
Closed shut, no entry
Matching pairs below have space enough
One gone completely
Wide open to rain, wind
And cobwebs
when it's still enough.

Lower down blacker, out of rain
Doors and shutters thick with grime,
Through them stored a picture still
Of bikes, machines, tools by a sign,
A bicycle shop where weary lads
Could mend then before the hill
Crossing the bridge once more
Taking them out of town

On the old bridge road
Where the mill stands
Alone but not forlorn
Hopeful still.

Topaz

Topaz sign bright lit
142 a litre if it's gas you want
beyond lines across the street
houses light and grey set at angles
a sole flag sagging
flaccid penis after yesterday's wind
no longer tall, erect
no more proudly shouting
it's Ireland here
and the west at that.

With the morning sun, calm makes limp
around spirits now lifted,
horizontal stripes, palest blue
where a gleaming cloud line moves
a gold patch true, small enough
with bird song now rain has gone
reminding all that spring is dressing
nearby, round the corner
beyond the hill and circle
arriving the day after another or so.

On the river

Birds are out in full force
calling the spring
a day late now, soft
rains accepted after heaving gales,
sole seagull leaves its mates
settling on the old railway bridge
used seldom, now silent
undisturbed further down the river,
while upstream the concrete bridge
looks slight though appearance deceives
an early stroller
umbrella high
off to church
or coffee with Sunday friends,

clouds seep in and out
reach blue fading to blonde foam
declaring sun is quite near
birds singing on and off
masked as traffic grows
this early Sunday morning
praising spring
as seagulls fly towards the place
they know best
a coastline painted clouds before us.

Rosscarbery memory

In loving memory, on the white cross
at the corner into town
though who remembers
>   the love and passion
>   the hope or resignation
>   sighs in the night
or beneath hedges in sunlight.

Memories of loving
lasting only in minds of the aged
gone cold with the years
buried deep in the soil
loneliness of earth's recollections
>   hidden, illicit secrets enjoyed
>   unknown, unsuspected
>   by stonemasons and town's youth.

Those memories of loveliness
sweet words whispered wildly
forbidden, recall innocence
life living the memory
those short moments of passion
>   loveliest moments of carefree years
>   love for a minute
>   these spirits of joy.

A voice

Wind through the hawthorn
whistling
>	or is it just the exhaust of a jet
>	sad
>	calling me
>	saying something of the past
a song
of hawthorn
with rosemary.

From Eavan Boland's 'Anna Liffey'

Life, the story goes,
Was the daughter of Canaan,
And came to the plain of Kildare.
She loved the flat-lands and the ditches
And the unreachable horizon.
She asked that it be named for her.
The river took its name from the land.
The land took its name from a woman…

Consider rivers.
They are always en route to
Their own nothingness. From the first moment
They are going home. And so
When language cannot do it for us,
Cannot make us know love will not diminish us,
There are these phrases
Of the ocean
To console us.
Particular and unafraid of their completion.
In the end
Everything that burdened and distinguished me
Will be lost in this:
I was a voice.

Eavan Boland, New Collected Poems, W.W. Norton, 2008

www.ingramcontent.com/pod-product-compliance
Lightning Source LLC
Chambersburg PA
CBHW050250120526
44590CB00016B/2285